FRACTURED LANDSCAPE QUILTS

KATIE PASQUINI MASOPUST

C&T PUBLISHING

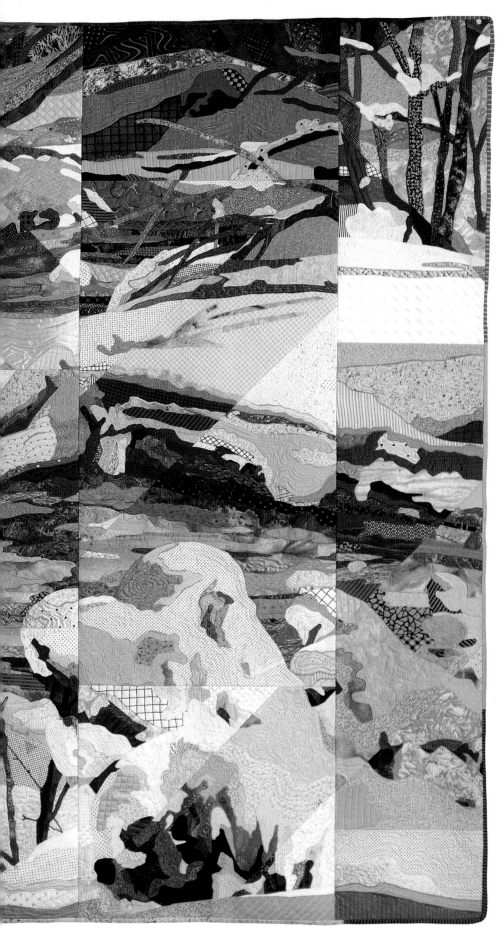

Rio Hondo, 80" x 54", by Katie. 1994.
From the collection of Jack Walsh III

The Rio Hondo is the river that runs down
toward Santa Fe, from the Taos ski basin.
The quilt started out very monochromatic,
lots of white with a little blue and brown.
Once the drawing was fractured I decided to
play Jack Frost and paint the landscape
different colors within the diagonal weaves.
This allowed me to play with many different
colors and added fantasy to the piece.

© 1996 Katie Pasquini Masopust
Editor: Lee Jonsson
Technical Editor: Diana Roberts
Hand Illustrator: Katie Pasquini Masopust
Electronic Illustrator: John M. Cram
Copy Editor: Judith M. Moretz
Book Design: Riba Taylor, Sebastopol, CA
Cover Design: Kathleen Lee and John M. Cram
Landscape photography: Katie Pasquini Masopust
All other photography: Hawthorne Studio, unless otherwise noted.

Pasquini Masopust, Katie
    Fractured landscape quilts / Katie Pasquini Masopust.
        p.   cm.
    Includes bibliographical references and index.
    ISBN 1-57120-016-9 (pbk.)
        1. Machine appliqué.   2. Machine quilting.   3. Quilts.   4. Fabric
pictures.   5. Landscape in art.   I. Title.
    TT779.P36   1996
    746.3--dc20   96-5563
                                                                       CIP

Published by C&T Publishing
P.O. Box 1456
Lafayette, CA 94549

Printed in Hong Kong
10   9   8   7   6   5   4   3   2   1

TABLE OF CONTENTS

DEDICATION

To my husband Bobby

ACKNOWLEDGMENTS

Bob Sr., for his support;
My great step kids, Jessi, Bobby III, and Brad;
Randi, who doesn't miss a thing;
Sherry Bradley, for our Thursday night session;
Don Gregg, for his brilliant photography;
Valerie at Bob's Sew & Vac, Albuquerque, NM,
    for her invaluable help when I was learning
    to machine quilt;
Pfaff Sewing Machine Company;
Joyce Drexler of Sulky, for introducing me to her
    tear away stabilizer;
Cindi and Dave at Technographics in Santa Fe,
    NM, for enlarging all my quilt patterns;
kinko's® in Santa Fe, for patiently doing all my
    heat transfers and teaching me to speak
    "Kinkese";
kinko's® all over the land, for enlarging my
    student works;
"The Outlaws," who I hold captive with my
    guns blazing.

Out of Darkness, 78" x 92", by Katie. 1984.
From the collection of Bob Masopust Sr.
Photograph by Lindsay W. Olsen.

PREFACE

I began painting as a child. I continued painting—with oils—until 1977, when I discovered quilting. I made several traditional quilts, learning the process and techniques. I started designing my own quilts based on a Mandala format. From there I made dimensional quilts, working with three-dimensional designs and isometric perspective. Throughout these series I would break from the geometric designs to do landscape quilts. The quilts shown on pages 6 and 7 are examples of my earlier unfractured landscapes.

In 1991 my husband and I moved to Santa Fe, New Mexico. I was very impressed with the area. The sky was the most clear turquoise, and the land was diverse and colorful. I was so inspired I completely changed my quiltmaking style. I have always done very dimensional, structured work, but the land called out to me and I saw quilts wherever I looked. I started going on what I call "quilt hunts," where I would drive around with my camera looking for quilt inspiration. Then I would draw the landscape from the photos.

I could not break totally with my structured nature, so on top of my landscape drawings I added lines and circles to break up the organic lines. The drawings then looked fractured, as if you were looking through broken glass. I then put these images to fabric. I became excited about the possibilities. I feel as if I have come full circle, returning to my painting; but this time I am painting with fabric and thread.

Redwood Tree at Sunset II, 72" x 108", by Katie. 1982. From the collection of Bob Masopust Sr. Photograph by Lindsay W. Olsen.

INTRODUCTION

DEFINITION

Fracture: to break, crack
Landscape: a view of scenery

Fracturing the landscape creates shapes and spaces in order to use a wider variety of fabrics, textures, and values. Fracturing adds a different dimension or surrealistic quality to the quilt, and can be used to quilt the piece in the "quilt-as-you-go" method.

I came to fractured landscapes through a slow process; it took several quilts to develop the method completely. My first landscape quilt was the *Rio Grande Gorge*. I was driving north to Taos from Santa Fe, crested the hill, and saw the Gorge, our own miniature Grand Canyon. I was so inspired; then and there I decided to do landscapes. I photographed the Gorge and then noticed the fabulous clouds floating by in the brilliant turquoise sky. I wanted to put these clouds in my quilt sky. Painting them into my quilts was not an option. (Clouds are the most difficult thing for me to paint.) I could, however, photograph them. I remembered being in a print shop that could put your family photo onto a T-shirt. Well, if they could put a photo onto a T-shirt, why couldn't they put a photo onto my own cotton fabric?

Rio Grande Gorge, New Mexico

Line drawing of *Rio Grande Gorge*

I drew the *Rio Grande Gorge* and was concerned about how I would get my cloud fabric, which was only eleven inches by seventeen inches, into the sky. Either my quilt was going to be very small or I would have to break the surface to allow parts of the clouds to be plugged into the sky.

I laid a piece of tracing paper over the drawing and made random lines with a ruler and compass. This was exciting because I could stay with my old structured style, while blending it with the organic line of the landscape. As you can see from the original drawing of the Gorge, there are large areas that would have been interpreted as single fabrics, but with the addition of the fractured lines I could use many different fabrics. In this first quilt the whole design was pieced as one top and then quilted by hand. I did several more pieces using this same method, drawing the landscape, fracturing the surface, sewing it all together, and hand quilting it.

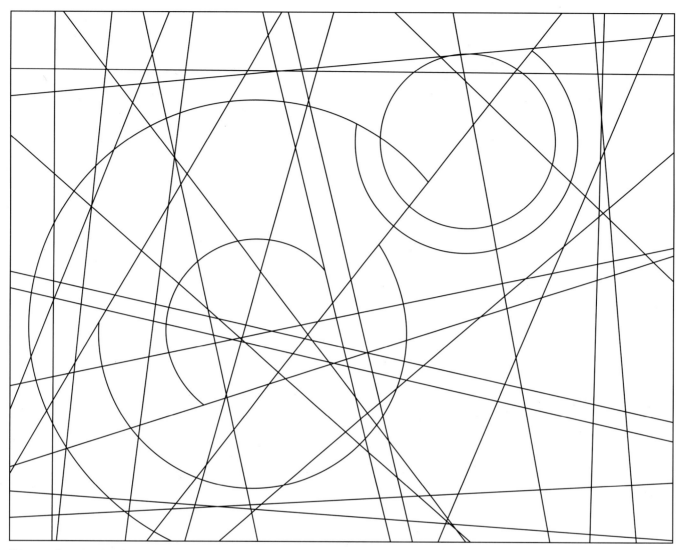

Fracture line drawing for *Rio Grande Gorge*

The fracture lines add interest, complexity, and balance to the simplicity of the design. Straight lines were drawn at random to create movement. Circles were added in three spots to enhance the composition and allow the eye to move freely around the piece. They seem to weave in and out of the landscape and the straight fracture lines.

My next big transition brought me to machine quilting. I saw in a show a prize-winning quilt that impressed me. It was a landscape, and you felt as if you were there. I analyzed what made this quilt so wonderful and realized it had millions of small pieces and tons of quilting. I said to myself, "Smaller pieces, more quilting."

My next photos were taken of a rock formation near my home. As I drew my landscape I was intrigued by all the smaller rocks that made up the larger formation. My drawing was quite detailed. I realized that with all its little pieces this would be much too thick to quilt through with my little #12 needles! So, I would have to machine quilt it.

Rio Grande Gorge, 64" x 50", by Katie. 1993.
From the collection of Wolfgang & Angelica Schmidt Lange

The line drawing of *Rio Grande Gorge* is very simple. The fracture lines add interest and make a more complex design that balances the simplicity. Lighter fabrics were used in the fractured circles as a suggestion of the sun. Cloud photo transfers were added in the sky.

My first thought was of the one bed quilt I had tried to machine quilt. I remembered my aching back and shoulders, and how frustrating it was. (One of my rules is that quilting must be fun.) I had a different goal in mind when I laid my tracing paper over my drawing to fracture it. If I was going to machine quilt it, I would have to do it in the method I used for my first Log Cabin quilt way back in 1979, "quilt-as-you-go."

The fracture lines would not only break the surface to allow me to use different color values as well as my cloud transfers, but would also allow me to put the quilt together in smaller pieces, quilt them, and then sew them all together. Quilting was so much fun in these smaller sections; you could spin and turn the piece, and do all sorts of wild things. Well, that was it for me. I haven't gone back to those little #12 needles since.

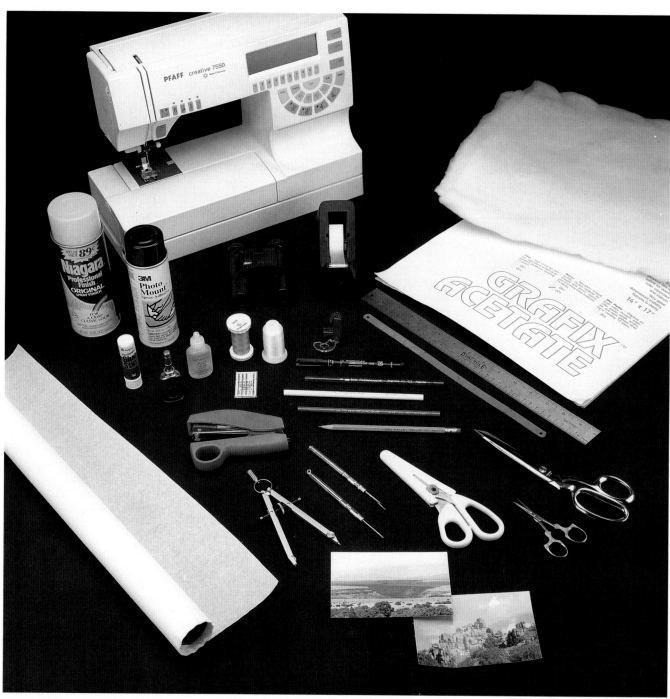

Supplies

SUPPLIES

These are the supplies you need to create a fractured landscape quilt.

Acetate: .005 mat acetate, for tracing the photograph (found at art supply stores)

Batting: 3 oz. wool batting, for its pliability when blocking the completed quilt

Binoculars: to view quilt in progress from a distance

Black fine point permanent marker: for drawing on the acetate

Camera: for taking pictures of the landscape

Colored pencils: for marking on fabrics

Compass: for making fracture lines

Fabric: a large variety of colors from light to dark

Glue stick: to attach small pieces of fabric

Monofilament thread: an invisible thread for machine appliqué

Railroad board: 6-ply cardboard for templates, found at art supply stores

Ruler: for making fracture lines

Scissors: for cutting templates and fabric

Sewer's Aid: a silicone product to lubricate the thread

Sewer's stiletto: for turning edges, pulling thread up, and removing the stabilizer

Sewing machine: one that is able to do a blind hem and a satin stitch

Spray Adhesive: to attach template copy to railroad board and to adhere top, batting and backing for machine quilting (found at art supply and camera stores)

Spray starch: to help keep edges sharp and in place

Stabilizer: Sulky Totally Stable® tear away stabilizer

Stapler: for stapling fabrics and templates to the pin-up wall

Tape: transparent and masking tape

Thread: many different colors of long-fiber threads

Tracing paper: to use for fracturing

Turning bar: ½" metal bar for turning back strips

THE PROCESS

This is an outline of the steps you will take to create a fractured landscape quilt.

1. **Selecting a Photograph:** Choose a photograph that is clear and easy to understand, one that has a focal point and good composition.

2. **Drawing the Landscape:** Using acetate and a fine-point permanent marker to trace the landscape, draw the "quilt" by enclosing all of the shapes that will eventually read as templates.

3. **Fracturing the Surface:** Lay tracing paper over the drawing and break the surface with lines and curves.

4. **Enlarging the Drawing:** Trace the fracture lines directly onto the acetate drawing of the landscape. Take the drawing to a blueprint shop to have it enlarged. Have three copies made.

   Template: One copy is spray mounted to the railroad board.
   Placement: One copy is stapled to the wall for placement.
   Foundation: One copy is to be used for tracing the stabilizer and re-marking the backs of each fractured section.

5. **Shading the Fractures:** Using copies of the tracing paper fracture drawing, shade the sections: light, medium, or dark. Use this as a map to select the fabric values.

6. **Sorting the Fabrics:** Sort fabrics by color into seven steps (described in chapter 6) from light to dark.

   For the light fracture sections use steps 1, 2, and 3.
   For the medium fracture sections use steps 3, 4, and 5.
   For the dark fracture sections use steps 5, 6, and 7.

7. **Marking the Templates:** Choose a fractured section. In pencil, mark each template as light, medium, or dark (by referring to the original drawing placed over the photograph). On the back of the fractured section make a line with a colored pencil to show the edge of the fractured piece. This will remind you to cut the fabric along this edge with a healthier seam allowance to accommodate the shrinkage caused from quilting, and also indicate which edge does not get turned under when pressing.

8. **Cutting It Out:** Cut out the shape from the railroad board. Lay the template upside down on the back of the fabric and mark. Cut the fabric around the mark adding a ¼" seam allowance (½" along the edge of the fractured section). Staple the template behind the fabric to the pin-up wall in its proper place.

9. **Turning the Edges:** Lay the stabilizer, smooth side up, on top of the foundation copy. Trace the edge and each line of the fractured section with a ballpoint pen. Spray starch the back of the fabric. Using a stiletto and iron, turn the edges over the railroad board template and press. Lay the piece in position on the stabilizer and touch with the tip of the iron to hold in place.

10. **Machine Appliqué:** Use the blind hem stitch and monofilament thread to secure all the fabric shapes. Tear away the stabilizer.

11. **Basting and Backing:** Spray baste the batting, backing, and top together on each of the fractured sections.

12. **Machine Quilting—Satin/Straight Quilting:** Set the machine to zigzag. For a straight stitch, set the stitch width to zero, then while stitching, vary the width to create texture. Quilt each fracture section to the edge.

13. **Assembling the Quilt:** Cut the foundation copy on the fracture lines and use these sections to re-mark the sewing lines on the back of the quilted section. Sew sections right sides together, press the seams open, and trim. Apply bias tape and hand sew in place over the seams.

14. **Labeling the quilt:** Make a label using a color photo copy of the original photo and have it heat set onto fabric. Sew it in place on the back of the quilt.

Chapter 1

SELECTING A PHOTOGRAPH

It would be nice if we all had the time to study with a professional photographer. However, another way to learn how to take photographs and use a camera is to look to your community college or adult education for an affordable class. I decided to take a class from Don Gregg, who does all the photography of my quilts. It was helpful in several ways. He taught me about composition, bracketing, and light, all of which I will use. The main thing I learned was that photography is exciting. I could just travel and photograph, but I'd rather make quilts. So I completed my lessons and now have more confidence in my picture-taking ability.

I have made quilts from photographs I have taken myself and from photographs taken by others which I have found in books. I have found the quilts made from photos I have taken myself turn out better. I feel I have a closer understanding of the place and know the details and the emotion of the scene better. If you do use a photo taken by someone else, be sure to give credit where credit is due. Always state this quilt is based on a photograph taken by "so and so," since it is that person's composition and vision you have borrowed to create your piece.

The place you photograph should be powerful and beautiful. You will be working with the scene for quite some time, so make sure you will not grow tired of it. The more meaningful the landscape, the more satisfying the quilt.

LET'S GET STARTED!

Pick a spot. I keep my eyes open for interesting subjects as I go about my daily routine. You might find something of interest on your drive into town or on a walk around a park. It is also fun to pick a national park where you can turn a photo session into a family outing. I had never been to the Grand Canyon. My husband and I went there and were blown away! All the pictures in all the books could not come close to the beauty of the real thing.

Wherever you choose to take your photograph, there are a few things about photography you should keep in mind.

The ocean at Asilomar Beach, Pacific Grove, California

COMPOSITION

Composition is the arrangement of objects or shapes. Good composition allows the viewer's eye to travel around the piece. Visual contrast is important. This can be provided with color, line, form, and/or shape. Strong lines of the land should bring your eye into the picture. Small, detailed areas should be balanced by larger areas, places for the eye to rest. For example, a detailed rocky mountain can be balanced with a calm sky; a busy patch of colorful flowers can be calmed with a green field or evergreen trees in the background; and hard, sharp rocks can be balanced with soft snow.

Canyon de Chelly: a view from the ridge. The soft edge from the lens forces the eye to the center. The big rocks in the foreground bring you into the photo, carrying your eye around the far cliffs, then rolling down the river to start again at the big rocks.

Canyon de Chelly: The eye is drawn in to the black hole at the bottom of the photo. It then searches out the details in the smaller rocks and moves over the large smooth surface on the right. The composition of the rock formation is balanced by the cool blue sky which provides interesting negative space.

This close-up of a rock formation reveals a different way of seeing the Canyon.

Original photo of Rio Hondo

Photo of Rio Hondo cropped to create a better composition

Take time to study the scene through the camera lens. Move the camera around until you have a balanced, pleasing picture. If you have a tele-photo lens, try it at different distances. Often a close-up of an outstanding rock formation or the sun reflecting off a lake is more interesting than a photo of the whole scene. The photograph I took of the Rio Hondo had a lot of evergreen trees in the background. For the quilt (pages 2 and 3), I cropped the photo to emphasize the river, the log, and the snow.

Putting the focal point in the center of a picture doesn't always work. I find the rule of thirds helpful. Divide the picture into thirds both ways to create nine sections. Place the focal point on one of the four intersecting lines. This will help to create a more pleasing composition.

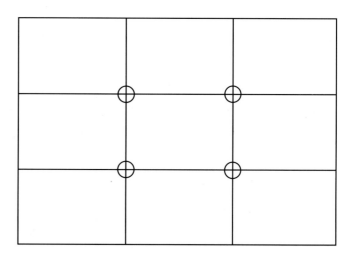

It is helpful to remember the "rule of thirds" when placing the focal point in your lens. Place the center of interest on any one of the intersections.

CLOSE-UPS FOR PHOTO TRANSFERS

I like to use lots of clouds in the sky areas of my quilts. Take photos of good, clear, distinct clouds. With some cameras, a polarizing filter will enable you to get greater detail from the clouds. This filter is attached to the lens, and by turning it you can see greater contrast. Take several photos of the same clouds, turning the filter a quarter turn each time. You will quickly learn which you like better. It is helpful to write down all your settings and turns as you are learning what your camera can do.

While you are photographing be sure to also take close-ups of rocks and sand, bark and leaves, or anything that would blend with the ready-made fabrics to give greater texture and realism to the final piece. These photographs can then be enlarged and heat transferred to fabric.

Detail of tree bark

Detail of pine needles

Photos of clouds taken when the polarizer is turned to let in the normal light

Detail of rocks

Photos of clouds taken when the polarizer is turned to filter the light to create greater detail

SELECTING THE PHOTOGRAPH

Choose a photograph that is clear and easy to understand, one that has a focal point and good composition, as well as variety in the shapes and sizes of the elements.

When you get your film back from the lab, look through the photographs and pull out the ones that are the most interesting and have the best light. The more contrast there is in your photo the greater the variety of contrasting fabrics you can use in your quilt to make it more interesting.

You may find you need to crop your picture to enhance the composition, or that you need to use different elements of several different photos. You may choose to go with a more abstract landscape. A detail of several rock outcroppings may be more interesting than the whole mountain. But use caution when choosing the abstract. If the photo is confusing and you can't really tell what you are looking at, it will only get more confusing when interpreted in fabric. That is not always bad, but you need to decide if that is how you want it portrayed. I chose to do a triptych of three rocks from a trip to Canyon de Chelly (pronounced *canyon du shay*). I had several good pictures of whole mountains, but decided to do a more abstract close-up. I wanted to portray the majesty of these finely chiseled rocks. (See the Canyon on pages 67–70.)

You will find some photos have poor composition or are uninteresting, but have the color you want. Pull these out to help choose your fabrics. If you are using color photo transfers, choose photos that are clear and have good color.

Redwood trees

Snowy river

Canyon de Chelly

These photos have poor composition but beautiful color. I pin these to my wall to inspire my color selections.

Chapter 2

DRAWING THE LANDSCAPE

Once you have decided on the photo, enlarge it to 8" x 10" or larger, as this will allow you to see more of the details. An enlargement from a negative is much clearer and easier to work with; however, a color photocopy enlargement will work if you do not have access to the negative.

Drawing for a quilt is a little different than drawing for a painting. Each shape must be enclosed. A shaded area can't be just "sketched" in; it must be seen as a complete and distinct shape. These drawings will become the templates when they are completed. This process of drawing the quilt can be done freehand or by tracing the photo. If traced, it must be done on a fairly transparent paper. Mat acetate .005 is the best.

Tape the acetate onto the photo and use a black fine-point permanent marker to draw the obvious shapes. These lines should be thin and dark, since they will only get thicker when the drawing is enlarged. Enclose each shape completely, then look for the dark shapes or shadows and trace them. Fill in the dark shapes. This will help clarify the drawing and aid in choosing fabrics later.

You can combine different elements from several photographs. First trace on the acetate whatever part you want in front, then lay down the next photo and trace the parts you want from it. This way you create your own composition when the one in the real world is not satisfactory. Be sure to keep the scale correct.

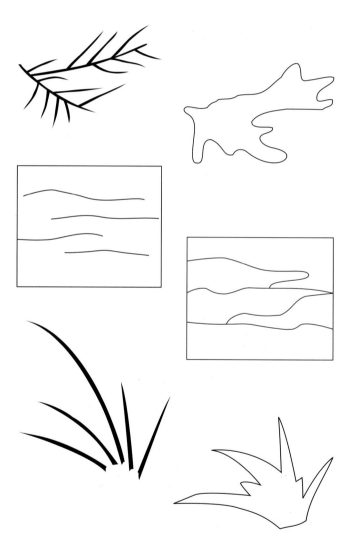

The illustrations on the left are drawings that won't work because they cannot be cut apart to create templates. The illustrations on the right are drawings that work because they are made up of complete shapes that can be cut apart to create templates.

Each step of tracing allows you to see the less obvious areas of light and dark. When you believe you are finished, look closer to see if there are any other shadows or color changes that need to be added. Little things like individual leaves, branches, or blades of grass will need to be drawn as complete shapes grouping the shadings together. If there are little branches or details too small to do in fabric, they can be done with satin stitch in the quilting process.

The more detailed the drawing is, the more impressive the quilt will be. Small pieces add the detail and, when combined with larger pieces, give balance to the design.

The drawing is the start of a long, involved project. Take time to give it the best possible start. Do not rush; spend several hours over several days. Enjoy the process; put on your artist's hat and play. It is a joy to see the vision come together.

The following images of *Picture Rock* and *Redwood Trees* show how the quilt was created by combining elements from different photographs. Study the *Redwood Trees* detail and drawing on page 29 to see how the shapes are drawn.

Opposite page, top:
The landscape drawing of *Picture Rock*

Bottom:
Picture Rock, 80" x 54", by Katie. 1994. From the collection of Angelica and Wolfgang Schmidt Lange

In order to create a pleasing composition I had to rearrange the composite photos of the actual scene. The overlapping photographs taped together gave me the idea for the fracture lines. Three values, light, medium, and dark, were used in the rectangles to give the illusion of different times of the day.

These two photos were placed closer together than the actual formations in order to create a better composition.

25

Three different photos taken at Richardson's Grove State Park in Northern California were overlapped to create *Redwood Trees*.

The complete drawing of *Redwood Trees*

Redwood Trees, 85" x 80", by Katie. 1995.
From the collection of Susan Cargill

When we were children our parents took us camping in the redwood forest several times every summer. There is nothing greater than these huge sequoias. I combined several shots to create this scene. As I was drawing the fracture lines I realized I couldn't find a way to create the streams of light with my fabrics, so I did it with my fracture lines, creating the diagonal slant of light weaving through the forest. The back of *Redwood Trees* shown on the following page reads as though you are looking at the back of the quilt.

Back of *Redwood Trees*

I continued the theme of the rays of light on the back using the same fabrics running through the rays. I used bold graphic fabrics in the circle sections for fun.

Detail of *Redwood Trees* drawing

Detail of *Redwood Trees*

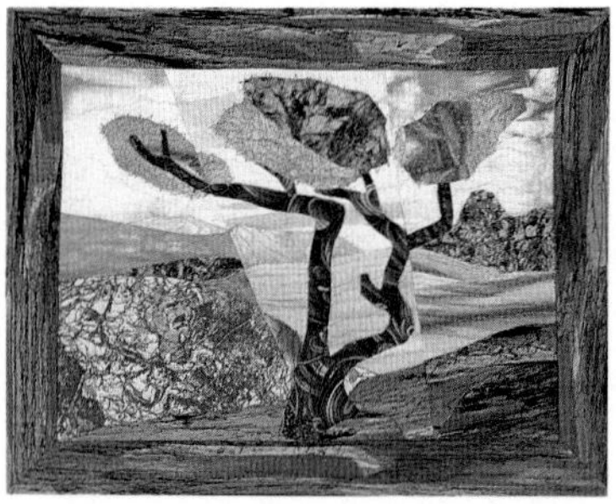

Chapter 3

FRACTURING THE SURFACE

Fracturing is the process of creating a series of lines that complement the drawing and fracture or "break" the surface, creating additional shapes. These new shapes allow for changes in color, value, and fabrics. They add a dimension that is not in the real landscape and enable you to machine quilt the piece in the "quilt-as-you-go" method. Each fractured section will be assembled as individual "blocks." When the sections are completed and quilted they will be sewn right sides together with the seam on the back. Then the seam will be covered with a strip of fabric to complete the back.

Fracture lines can be made with a ruler, a compass, or can be drawn freehand as organic lines. The easiest way to understand fracturing is to imagine you are looking through broken glass. Fracture lines should not break up individual sections but cross the entire surface. The lines are used to break up large areas and should run across the entire surface. Fracture lines should not be placed directly over a line in the original drawing.

Lay tracing paper over the landscape drawing and play with different configurations. It is best to sketch several possibilities quickly to free yourself. When the tracing paper is removed from the landscape it should be a good design all by itself. It is as if two different drawings are merged to create the fractured landscape. The tree quilts on the following pages show four different fracture designs.

Elements of the landscape can be used in designing the fracture lines. An underwater scene could be fractured with flowing lines representing the currents, an old adobe church could be fractured with lines in the shape of a cross, and a redwood forest could be fractured with lines representing sunlight streaming through the trees. (See *Redwood Trees* on page 27.)

Circles are very pleasing to use as fracture lines, but quarter-circles and definite half-circles are awkward looking. Circles are most effective when off-center and when they weave in and out of other fracture lines or each other.

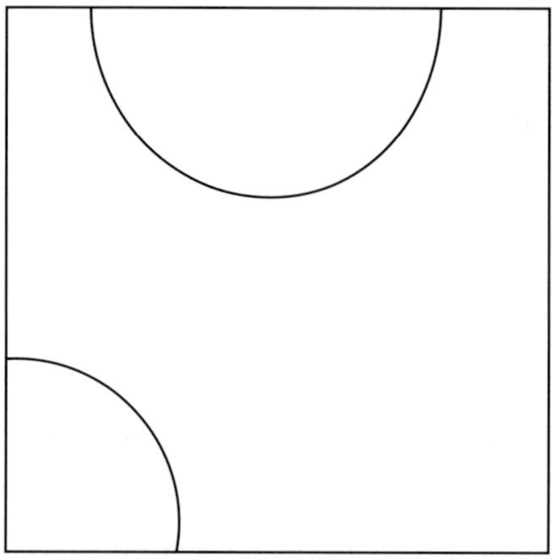

It is harder to make quarter-circles and half-circles work in the design.

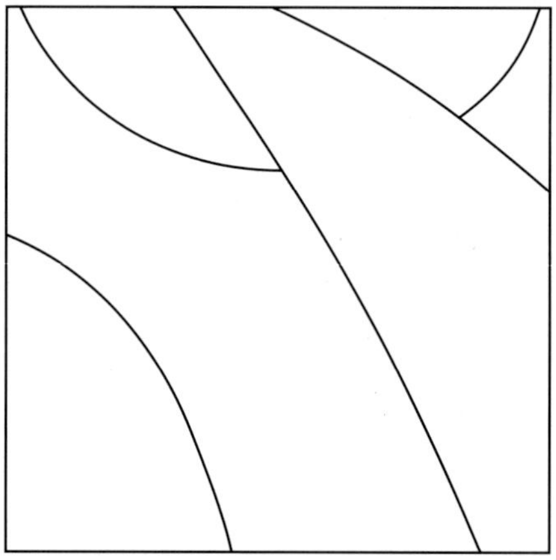

Circles are most effective when off-center and when they weave in and out of other fracture lines or each other.

Photo of the tree used in the tree quilt series

Line drawing of the tree

I like to think about how to fracture the surface for several days before I actually put pencil to paper. Each morning as I take my walk I reflect on my trip and my photographs of the area. I think about the shapes and feelings of my experience. Different possibilities come to mind. Eventually my thoughts lead me to a solution. When my landscape drawing is completed I set aside a block of time to play with my fracture ideas. Usually the problem is solved in one sitting.

You will know when the fractures are right because they will tell you so. There will be a good feeling of flow and movement between the landscape and the fracture. If you are unsure, wait a while and then try some other possibilities. You may also want to ask your friends for suggestions. The right solution will eventually stand out and you can proceed.

Different fracture drawings used for the tree quilts

Natural Tree

Black and White Tree

Electric Tree

Sunset Tree

Natural Tree, 36" x 48", by Katie. 1995.
From the collection of Sharon & Dan May

This is the first in a series of four tree quilts. I took a picture of this tree in Shakertown, Kentucky. I decided to portray it in four different colorways with four different fracture designs. The tree was drawn and used in the four different quilts. This first quilt was done using realistic colors.

Black and White Tree, 36" x 48", by Katie. 1995.
From the collection of Janet Sorell

I have always collected black and white fabrics and love to use them; so this was a perfect interpretation of the tree. The blacks and whites are treated as positives and negatives, alternating in each fractured section. If the tree is against a black fractured section, then the tree is white and vice versa.

Back of *Natural Tree*

Back of *Black and White Tree*

Electric Tree, 36" x 48", by Katie. 1995.
From the collection of Cathy Shanahan

I chose to do a very bold and bright tree
where complementary colors were used.
For example, if the tree was against a
blue sky, then the tree was the complement of blue, which is orange.

Sunset Tree, 36" x 48", by Katie. 1995.
From the collection of Bob Masopust, Sr.

The *Sunset Tree* was the perfect way to
end this series. I love sunsets not only
because they are beautiful, but also
because they allow me to use so many
different colors.

Back of *Electric Tree*

Back of *Sunset Tree*

Chapter 4

ENLARGING
THE DRAWING

The most accurate and efficient way to enlarge the drawing is to have it done professionally by a blueprint shop. Projecting the image onto paper and drawing the landscape on the wall three times is very time consuming (and all of the blood flows out of your fingers).

Trace the fracture lines onto the acetate. Decide how large the quilt will be. Make two arrows to show the printer the edge of the drawing, the actual edges you want enlarged. Indicate how large you want the enlargement between the arrows. For example, the drawing is 11" wide and you want the quilt to be 80" wide. The printer at the blueprint shop can enlarge your drawing to the desired size.

Call around to find the best place and check the prices. Always ask how much distortion you will get on the copies. If it is over ½" you will find it difficult to line up the fracture lines. You are looking for a place that has a 36"-wide enlarging machine. They will have to enlarge the drawing initially by two hundred percent. Then depending

on the complete size needed they will send it through several times, giving you several lengths 36" wide by the length you have determined, until the full size is attained. There will be an overlap for placement. Many Kinko's are equipped to do this, and their copies are accurate enough if either the height or width will only be 36 inches.

Enlarging will run anywhere from $20 to $75 depending on the desired size. I balance this cost with the realization that it would have taken me several days, if not more, to draw the redwoods three times. The print shop took an hour and I sang all the way home. Remember, time is money.

You will need three copies. The first is the template copy; this one must be accurate. The second is the placement copy, to put on your pin-up wall for placement. (It is not important for this copy to be accurate. It is just for placement while cutting out the fabrics. This can be made on a 36"-wide copy machine.) The third is the foundation copy; this copy must be accurate.

Place arrows at the edges you want enlarged to your desired size.

Tip: Have the blueprint shop make the two accurate copies directly from the original drawing. Photocopy the third copy from the accurate enlargement.

Template copy: Tape together pieces of 22" x 28", 6-ply railroad board. (Railroad board is thin enough to cut with scissors, but thick enough to mark around as a template.) Lay the pieces on the floor side by side and tape the whole length of the seams. Do this until the surface is as large as the pattern. Leave the taped side up. This way all the tape will be between the railroad board and the paper pattern and will not melt onto your iron.

Using a spray adhesive, attach the template copy to the railroad board. Starting at one edge, spray about twelve to eighteen inches and roll the paper onto the railroad board, smoothing out all the air bubbles. Continue until the entire paper pattern is in place. If the design is over 36" and there are two paper rolls for the pattern, repeat the process, checking to see that the overlap matches and the pattern will read true. Trim the outside edge and cut into fractured sections.

Spray the cardboard evenly and smooth the paper pattern into place.

Placement copy: Staple this copy to the pin-up wall and staple the fractured sections of the template copy in place to keep everything in order.

Foundation copy: Put this copy away somewhere safe; it will be used later with the stabilizer.

Switzerland, 62" x 30", by Katie. 1996.

This black and white, negative-positive, abstract landscape quilt is based on a photo I took out the back door of a friend's house during my teaching visit to Switzerland. I enlarged my 10" drawing to three 62"-wide copies.

Chapter 5

SHADING
THE FRACTURES

The fractured sections can be seen as different values of light, medium, and dark, or used only to change fabrics and not values. When the fractured sections are of different values, make several reduced photocopies of the fracture design to experiment with shading. Try several different possibilities to determine which is best. Light sections will represent the brightest of sunlight; medium sections, the middle of day; and dark sections, twilight.

Fill in the dark sections with a black felt-tip pen, the medium sections with a pencil, and leave the light sections blank. The different shades should be balanced, and enhance the composition by helping the eye travel across the whole piece.

It is almost as if you are making a checkerboard, only you are using three shades. You don't want two fractured sections of the same shade touching, if possible. Start at the focal point with light, then hop around with light, medium, and dark, trying to balance them. Try other shading possibilities starting at the focal point with medium, and then with dark. Lay out each of the possibilities and choose the one that is most pleasing.

For *Rio Hondo* (shown on pages 2 and 3 with detail below) I shaded the diagonal weaves using many different colors which added fantasy to the piece.

Shading map of *Rio Hondo* showing the placement of color in the diagonal weaves

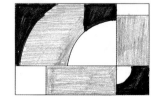

These shading maps show several different ways to shade the fracture sections for the project, Seasons, on page 90.

Detail of *Rio Hondo*

Chapter 6

SORTING THE FABRICS

There are three basic sets of colors needed for fractured landscape quilts: blues for sky and water; browns for dirt, rocks, and trees; and greens for foliage. (Brown includes many colors, such as pinks, reds, purples, oranges, etc.) Additional colors can be added depending on the elements in your photo.

Sort the fabrics into seven graduated steps from light to dark (Katie's Seven Step Program). Lay the fabrics into seven stacks. Step 1 will be white and very pale colors. Step 7 will be blacks and very dark colors. Steps 2-6 will be the value gradations between steps 1 and 7. Three sets are used for the different values of the fractured sections. Steps 1, 2, and 3 will be the light sections, with 1 being light, 2 being medium, and 3 being dark; steps 3, 4, and 5 will be the medium sections, with 3 being light, 4 being medium, and 5 being dark; and steps 5, 6, and 7 will be the dark sections, with 5 being light, 6 being medium, and 7 being dark. (Generally, steps 6 and 7 are good for water, but are too dark for a sky and make it appear gloomy, unless you are doing a night scene or storm.)

These seven steps can be stored in boxes, on shelves, or as I do, in seven sets of wire storage shelves. This storage system keeps all my fabrics organized and minimizes the sorting I have to do at the beginning of each new quilt

The color bands on the next four pages will help you sort your fabrics into the seven steps. Use the values shown here to sort other colors as well.

project. I simply file in new fabrics as I buy them. When you sort your fabrics in this manner you will notice where you have the fewest fabrics. They are usually steps 1, 2, 6, and 7. We are always tempted to buy the fabrics from the middle range because they are the most exciting colors; however, it is also important to have the light lights, the dark darks, and lots of good blacks, too.

The wire storage shelves I use to organize the Seven Step Program

The steps are staggered so when all the colors are open for light (1, 2, 3) I can see all the drawers.

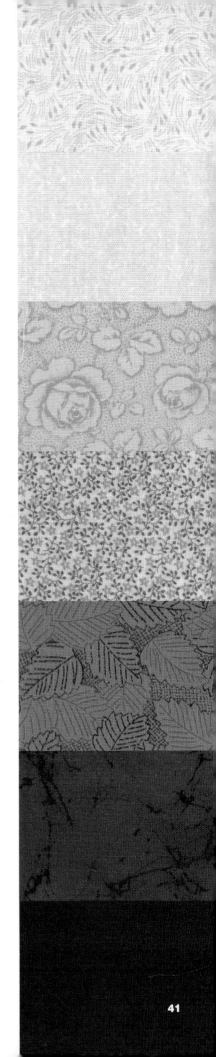

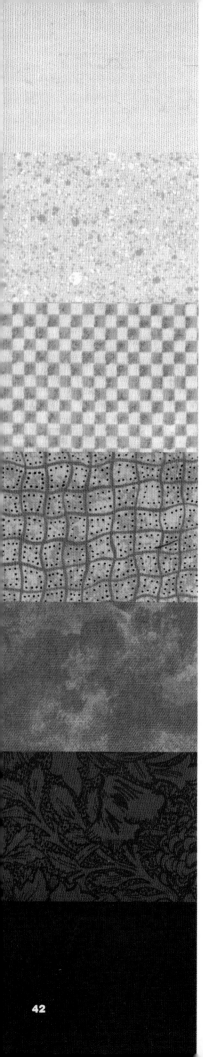

COLOR HEAT TRANSFERS

This process places the image of a photograph onto fabric. Oftentimes this technique is used to create family album quilts. In fractured landscapes it is used to create realistic textured fabric to enhance the scene and blend with ready-made prints and solids. Some of the things to transfer are clouds for the sky, pebbles for a beach, leaves for a tree, flowers for a meadow.

A clear photograph is needed; a 3" x 5" photo is fine. Take the photograph to a copy store that has a color copier. The printer can enlarge the photo directly onto transfer paper. Several photos can be grouped together on one page, or one photo can be enlarged to the full size of the paper. Use 11" x 17" transfer paper (8½" x 11" is often not large enough for the templates). Ask the copy store to lighten the image by one and a half steps because the image will darken when heat-set to fabric.

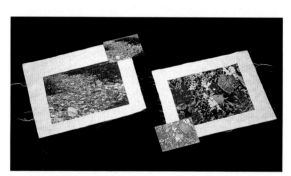

Transfer fabric of close ups

There are so many wonderful fabrics on the market. Use as many as you can to create a diverse, rich texture. Combine solids, calicos, tie-dyes, air brush, wild prints—anything and everything. I use fine, dark velveteen for the darkest dark. It absorbs one hundred percent of the light and gives dimension to the dark areas. I love to use fabrics that would not traditionally be considered landscape fabrics, such as checks, stripes, and graphic prints. Color heat transfer photocopies on fabric can also be used to create your own textures. I especially like the heat transfers for clouds in the sky areas.

The transfers need to be heat set onto fabric that is cut slightly larger than the transfer paper. One hundred percent cotton or cotton blends work fine. Satin can also be used if it is the thin satin; bridal satin is too thick and becomes very stiff when a transfer is applied. White-on-white prints give an interesting texture when combined with the texture of the photo. Even small black prints on a white background will show through to create variety.

Transfer fabric of clouds

Cloud transfers printed on textured fabrics

Take the fabric and the heat transfer to a T-shirt shop and have them heat press it together. Treat these transfers as regular fabric and file them into the seven steps.

There are beautiful large print fabrics on the market. Those with different colors and values are hard to force into one of the seven steps. I have another drawer for these fabrics and try to remember to look there for that special texture or color.

I have found this way of sorting invaluable. After many years of fabrics strewn everywhere in my studio, and many hours wasted looking for the right piece, I now have faith in the Seven Step Program and trust my "drawers." I find I can work much faster, or at least with a greater sense of "flow," when I am not wasting time determining which value each fabric is.

Chapter 7

MARKING THE TEMPLATES

Begin by choosing a fractured section from the placement copy on the wall. In pencil, mark each template shape with an L for light, M for medium, or D for dark (unless the dark areas have already been filled in). This is done by laying the acetate over the original photo and determining the different shades. If there are different colors used and it is not apparent from the shapes which is which, you may indicate the color where necessary.

Draw a line in colored pencil around the edge of the entire fractured section on the back. This will indicate the edges of the fracture section, which when cut into little pieces for the templates will require a larger seam allowance.

Marking a colored line on the back of the fracture section

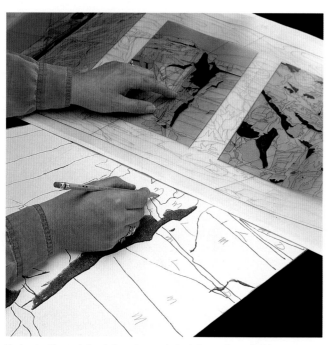

Refer to the original drawing to label the values light, medium, or dark (L, M, or D) on the templates.

The circle areas of *Perklo Park* were shaded in steps 3, 4, and 5 adding black for the shadows to create high contrast, while the background was done in low contrast.

Photo of Perklo Park

The complete drawing of *Perklo Park*

I didn't want the fracture lines to break up the building so I chose to fracture in large circles to emphasize the three points of interest.

Perklo Park, 54" x 34", by Katie. 1996.
From the collection of Randi and Mike Perkins.

I was commissioned by my friends, Randi and Mike, to make a quilt of their home. At first I was reluctant to make a quilt of a house; but as you can see, not much of the actual house shows. Randi has a green thumb and her house is like a garden.

Detail of *Perklo Park*

Back of *Perklo Park*

Chapter 8

CUTTING IT OUT

Check the shading map to see what value (light, medium, or dark) the fracture section is. Choose a fabric from the appropriate step to match the value indicated on the template. Within each fractured section are light, medium, and dark templates. If you are working with a light section from the shading map, choose fabrics from steps 1, 2, and 3. For medium sections, choose fabrics from steps 3, 4, and 5. For dark sections, choose fabrics from 5, 6, and 7.

While you are working with a section, pull out the three drawers or put sticky labels on only those stacks you are using. Once you are finished using a piece, return the remaining fabric to the back of the proper drawer or stack to make sure you don't use the same print for a while. This forces you to use a variety of fabrics and keeps you from using your favorites over and over again. The more fabrics you use, the richer your quilt will look.

Cut the individual shapes (templates) from the railroad board as you use them. I use three-inch scissors because they are small and turn easily for those convoluted shapes.

Lay the template upside down on the back of the fabric. Mark the sewing line and cut, eyeballing a quarter of an inch bigger.

Cut individual shapes for the templates.

Mark around the template on the back of the fabric.

If the edge with the colored line is shown on the template, draw a line out into the fabric to remind you to cut a healthier seam allowance. This will make the whole section larger to accommodate the quilting, which makes the fractured section shrink.

Cut the fabric by eyeballing ¼" bigger all around the drawn line; cut the edge side bigger to allow for shrinkage.

Pin or staple the fabric with the template behind it to the placement copy on the pin-up wall. Continue in this manner until all of the fabrics are cut. When all the pieces are positioned on the wall, take a reducing glass or the wrong end of binoculars and study the design. Make sure everything looks right and you are happy with the way the secondary fractured pattern is emerging.

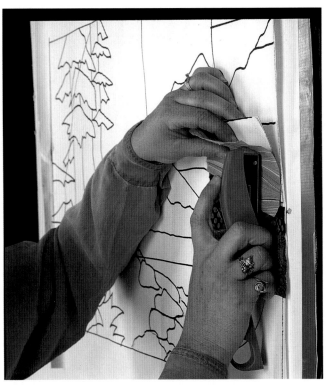

Place the template behind the fabric and staple them both to the foundation copy on the wall.

It may be difficult to see what is happening with all the overlapping fabric pieces stapled to the wall. Some people prefer working with one fractured section at a time, cutting all the pieces out, folding the edges under, and attaching them to the stabilizer before moving on to the next section. I like to complete one step at a time, cutting *everything* out before I go on to the next step. It is much easier to change something before it is sewn. But it really is a matter of preference.

MARKING PENCILS

I like to use four different marking pencils. I use white to mark on the very dark fabrics; lead pencil to mark on the very light fabrics; a red, or "warm" colored pencil, to mark on "cool" fabrics; and a green, or "cool" colored pencil, to mark on "warm" colored fabrics.

All the pieces stapled to the wall

Chapter 9

TURNING THE EDGES

Return to the pattern's foundation copy. Make reference marks with a colored pencil where one fracture line meets another and three or four inches apart along the curve. These reference marks will be transferred later to the back of the fractured sections for easy assembly.

Use a stabilizer to align all the pieces before they are sewn. The Sulky product Totally Stable®, an iron-on tear away stabilizer, works best. The Sulky stabilizer uses heat to hold the pieces in place.

Lay the stabilizer, smooth side up, on top of the foundation copy. Trace the edge and each line of the fractured section with a ballpoint pen. Add a ½" seam allowance to the outside edge of the fractured section to accommodate the shrinking when it is quilted.

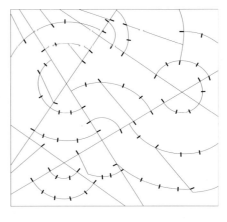

Transfer reference lines: where lines meet other lines and along the curves.

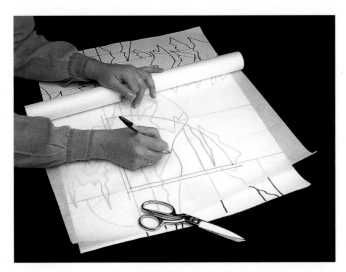

Stabilizer is placed smooth side up over the foundation copy. Ballpoint pen is used to transfer all lines.

To begin the next step of turning the edges under, remove a fabric with its template from the design wall. You can start from any side (top, bottom, left, right) and work your way across the fractured section. Use the following guidelines to help you determine which edges need to be turned under.

■ Any edges that will be under another shape should be left flat.

■ Objects that appear in the foreground of your photo don't necessarily have to be appliquéd on top of the "background" shapes.

■ Check the shapes you have already attached to the stabilizer to see which edge on the next shape should be turned under.

■ If the edge you need to turn under is too convoluted, use the "triple whammy" technique described on page 51.

Spray starch the fabric on the wrong side. Lay the template upside down onto the back of the fabric, aligning it with the sewing lines. Clip the inside curves. Pull the fabric over the template and toward the iron using a stiletto as you press. The sewer's stiletto will save your fingers from burns.

If you are right handed, hold the stiletto in the left hand and the iron (set to steam) in the right. Hold the stiletto as you would the top chopstick. Use your little finger to ground your hand to the ironing board and hold the template in place.

Place the edge to be folded over away from you and pull the fabric toward you and into the iron. Rotate the piece as needed. Hold the iron on the fabric for a few seconds to allow the spray starch to completely dry, or "cook," the fabric. If the spray starch is still damp when the iron is removed, the pressed edge may not stay in place.

Remove the cardboard and tape it to the foundation copy for reference. Later, if you need to change a color or fabric, you can find the template easily.

Proper way to hold stiletto

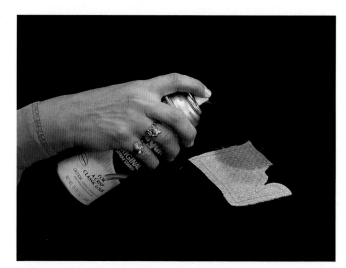

Spray starch fabric on the back.

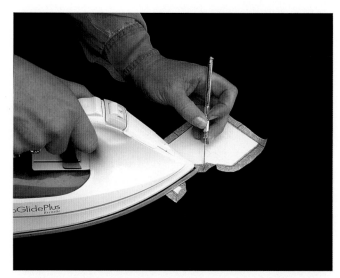

Folding edges over the template with the iron and stiletto

POINTS

Points are handled by folding the edge over across the point, then rotating and folding the other edge over the point, creating a "flag" that shows on the first side. Clip this excess fabric off, since it will be secured when it is machine appliquéd in place.

Spray starch, turn one side over the template, then turn and press the other side over creating a "flag" at the point. Clip the flag to create a sharp point.

DIFFICULT FABRICS

Many beautiful fabrics you may want to use in your quilt can't handle the heat of the iron. These include lamé, acetate, heat transfers, and some blends. Lamé does not fray, so the easiest way to treat it is to cut on the sewing line and avoid turning the edges, or place it on the bottom and turn the surrounding pieces under. The latter is the best solution for the other delicate fabrics as well. For these fabrics I also cut on the line and glue stick in place. I used this method for the branches on the four tree quilts.

If you have other difficult fabrics that fight being turned under, such as tapestries, you can treat them with a "triple whammy" of spray starch. Spray the offending fabric and iron it dry. Turn the fabric over, spray, and iron it again. Draw around the template and spray the wrong side of the fabric one more time. Carefully cut on the line and glue stick in place.

It is likely there will be fine points or turns where there is not enough seam allowance to fold both sides under. When this occurs, cut directly on the sewing line of one side. This side will have no edge turned under and the other edge will have the seam allowance turned under. The edges without a seam allowance will be held in place with decorative satin stitches when quilted.

Tip: Spray starch can cause quite a buildup on your ironing board cover. I do all the spray starching at the small end of the board and I have a washcloth handy to wipe off the starch each time. The combination of spray starch and the heat of the iron will cause the ironing board cover and light colored fabrics to discolor as you press them. To avoid the discoloring, cut a length of white fabric approximately eight inches wide and pin or staple it to the existing cover. Do all your pressing on the white fabric. It will be obvious when it discolors and you can move to a clean spot.

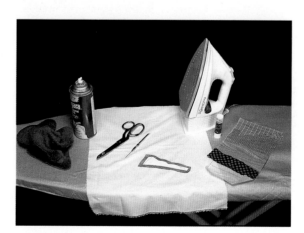

Ironing board set up for turning edges

I have found that many of the template pieces look the same. I revert to my younger days as a jigsaw puzzle enthusiast since the tracing lines on the stabilizer are not always easy to relate to the actual template. By referring to the foundation copy I can assure myself that a certain piece does indeed belong where I put it. If a piece is missing it may not be apparent from the stabilizer, but will certainly show on the foundation puzzle.

Lay the pressed fabric in place onto the stabilizer and touch it with the tip of the iron to bond it with the stabilizer. (Use a glue stick to attach any pieces where there is no stabilizer showing, or to attach fabrics that could be damaged by the heat of the iron.) When positioning pieces onto the stabilizer you need to place them somewhere near the lines. However, it is not important to get everything perfect. It is difficult to see the lines when a few of the pieces are in place, and because this is fractured it is not important to have everything "match." Remember, fracturing is like looking through broken glass; everything is a little "off," creating that broken look. It is actually better if the rocks, the mountains, or other elements used in the design don't match exactly when the fractured sections are sewn together. How nice not to "match."

Continue on in this manner until all the pieces of the fractured section are in place. When all the pieces are tacked in place, carefully turn the whole thing over and press the entire surface lightly to hold everything securely while sewing. Do not press too hard or the stabilizer will be difficult to remove. Do this for each section.

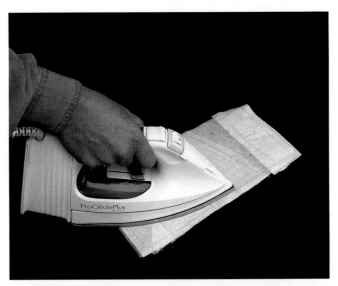

Lightly press the back of the stabilizer to secure all the pieces.

Pin the sections back to the wall. Study the piece carefully. Make sure the secondary pattern is emerging and the flow of colors is right. It is much easier to change it now than after it is sewn. If you need to change a color or fabric, find the template that has been taped to the foundation copy, cut a new piece, and exchange it. When everything is perfect, hand or machine appliqué in place one fractured section at a time.

Attach fabric to the stabilizer with the tip of the iron.

MACHINE APPLIQUÉ

Like previous steps, you will machine appliqué one fractured section at a time, working across the piece from one side to the other. Use the blind hem stitch on the sewing machine with transparent or monofilament thread on the top and neutral-colored thread in the bobbin to appliqué the pieces in place. Set the blind stitch setting for a short length and a small bite. On some machines, use the double needle to make the bite small enough.

Test to see that the bottom thread does not show. If it does, loosen the top tension or tighten the bobbin tension slightly. (There will always be a little dot of color that will show.) If you don't have the blind hem setting on your machine, a small zigzag will work.

The length of the stitch is run on the bottom fabric right along the edge of the top pieces, with the bite going into the top piece.

As you appliqué the pieces in place there will be areas that are not turned under. (See explanation for turning edges under in the previous chapter.) Appliqué over these edges as you would for the turned edges. When machine quilting, these areas will be more firmly attached with a satin stitch.

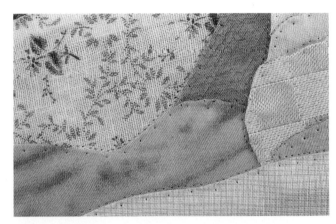

Detail of blind hem with stitching along the side of the folded edge with the straight stitch going into the bottom fabric and the bite into the top fabric

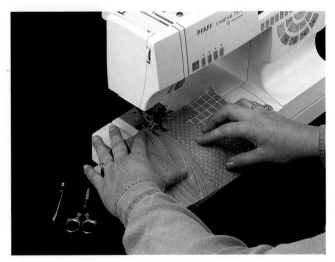

Use an open foot so you can see the edge and sew carefully.

HAND QUILTING

If you choose to hand quilt, the fractured sections will be used to change fabrics and create pattern. The entire surface will be pieced as one and quilted as a whole. At this point you should determine if you would like to add any satin stitching to embellish the top. This can add detail and also cover any unturned edges or sloppy points.

After all the top stitching is done, sew the fractured sections together along the seamline of the stabilizer. When all the fractured sections are together, tear away the stabilizer. Try to get as much off as possible. Cut the batting and backing about an inch bigger all the way around. Baste and hand quilt the layers.

Sunset at the Grand Tetons, 60" x 50", by Katie. 1993.

This quilt was hand quilted. The line drawing for the sky and the reflection is complicated, with many small pieces. Very few fracture lines were used. Three sets of concentric circles were created to weave in and out of the mountains. Each concentric circle was translated in a different value with the same configuration reflected in the lake.

Fractured Silhouette, 66" x 48", by Katie. 1993.
From the collection of Dena Canty

This piece was hand quilted. The drawing of the dead branch is organic and flowing. I chose the hard edges of a traditional isometric pattern to fracture the large sky area. Light, medium, and dark were kept in their proper isometric position. The branch is also broken at the isometric edge. The turquoise pieces were used as foundations, the black for the branch was appliquéd on each individual isometric shape, then the turquoise was trimmed from behind.

MACHINE QUILTING (QUILT-AS-YOU-GO)

For the "quilt-as-you-go" method, you need to decide if all the fracture lines will be kept as they are on the front. If you have a lot of small sections, they can be sewn together to create larger sections to quilt. Some of the fractured sections of the *Grand Canyon* shown on the next page were sewn together to create larger sections to machine quilt. (See mock-up of back on page 58.) Sew these right sides together along the seamline and then tear away all the stabilizer. Use the stiletto to separate the fabric from the stabilizer and tear away as much as possible from the seams. Some will be left under the stitches, but if too much is left, it will be tough on the needle when quilting.

Removing the stabilizer is my least favorite step. I find it twice as frustrating when I do it in a hurry. Knowing this about myself has led me to save this particular step for a special time. I work in my studio from very early in the morning until my husband comes home from work. I find it difficult to work accurately and enjoyably after about 6:00 p.m., with or without a husband. I save this chore for after dinner, when my husband and I enjoy each other's company watching TV or discussing our day. I place a grocery bag by my end of the couch, relax, and remove stabilizer piece by piece.

Tear away as much of the stabilizer as possible.

Photo of Grand Canyon

Fracture map of *Grand Canyon*

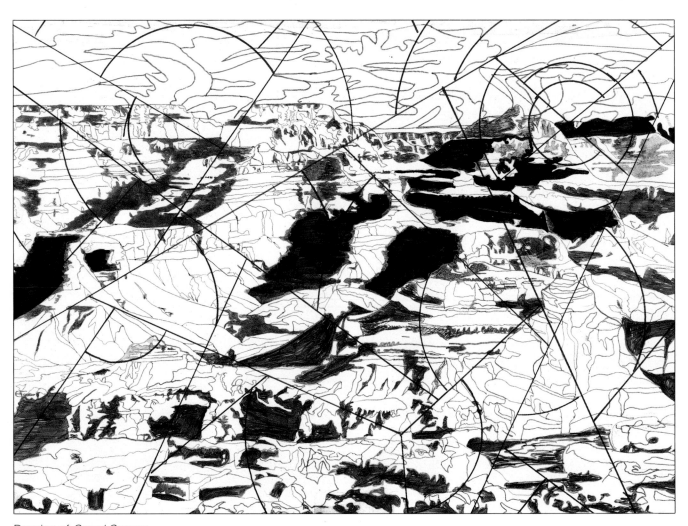

Drawing of *Grand Canyon*

Grand Canyon, 85" x 65", by Katie. 1995.
From the collection of the Hendricks

I have seen many photos of the Grand Canyon, but I was
never so impressed as when I looked over the canyon early
one morning. Photos do not do it justice; you have to see
the Grand Canyon to know it. I love the way it appears there
are two quilts here at one time. At first the light, medium,
and dark fracture sections create a wonderful dance. Then
as you look deeper the mountains and valleys appear and
disappear, doing their own little dance.

Chapter 11

BASTING AND BACKING

The fracture sections create an interesting pattern on the back of the quilt. It is helpful to have a map of the back to aid in choosing fabrics. Trace only the fracture lines. (If there are many small sections or subfractures, use the larger fracture). Turn the tracing paper over and make a paste-up of the fabrics for each section.

The fabrics to use on the back can be wild prints, as in *Picture Rock*, or softer prints, as in *Rio Hondo*, to show the machine quilting. Fabrics for the back of *Grand Canyon* were chosen for their worn-out look, and were further enhanced by spraying with bleach to give them that "found at the bottom of the canyon" look.

As you take a fractured section from the wall, refer to the map and choose the appropriate backing fabric. Cut this fabric and the batting about an inch bigger than the front all the way around. I like to use a wool batting because it is easier to quilt and block.

Use a spray adhesive to baste these fractured sections. Line up the backing onto the batting. Fold half the backing back to expose the batting. Lightly spray the batting with spray adhesive. Gently smooth the backing onto the sticky batting. Fold the other half of the backing back and spray the rest of the batting. Then turn it over and do the same thing to the other side, spraying the batting and smoothing the appliquéd top in place.

Mock-up of *Grand Canyon* back

Mock-up of *Redwood Trees* back

Press the fractured section from the back to flatten all layers. This method eliminates any chance the machine quilting will create wrinkles on the back.

Spray adhesive can be purchased from any camera shop or artist supply store. Use the spray adhesive in a well ventilated room or outside, if possible. As the pieces are quilted and worked the spray adhesive will dissipate. Do not spray directly onto the fabric; it may discolor it.

Spray basting will only work for small quilts or on "quilt-as-you-go" pieces. A large quilt requires too much handling, and the spray will dissipate before you can quilt it all.

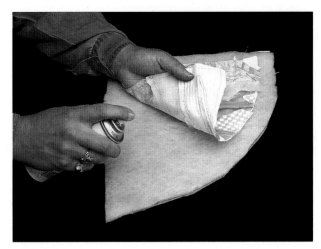

Lightly spray mount the batting and smooth on the back and top from the center out.

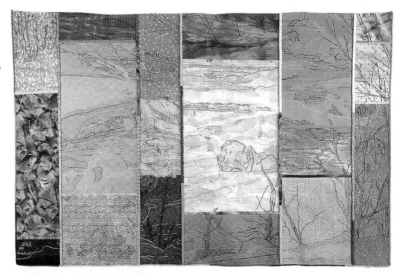

Back of *Rio Hondo*

Softer fabrics show the quilting stitches.

Back of *Picture Rock*

This was my first machine quilted piece. The wild prints helped hide my beginning stitches.

Chapter 12

MACHINE QUILTING

I add texture and interest to my quilt with free-motion Satin/Straight machine quilting. It is demanding and requires a well-serviced machine capable of smoothly changing from a zero width to a wide zigzag.

Use the darning foot that comes with your machine, or purchase a Big Foot™ made especially for free-motion quilting. Free-motion quilters usually lower the feed dogs. I prefer to leave the feed dogs up. This gives a little bit of friction and helps carry the pieces along, even in free-motion. Practice varying the width of the satin stitch from a straight stitch to the widest zigzag and back to a straight stitch again. This gives a nice texture to the top; the same width continuously looks chunky and awkward.

Aside from its decorative applications, one of the practical uses of satin stitching is to secure places where there is no seam allowance turned under. The satin stitch holds these areas in place and covers the raw edge. Satin stitching can also add thin branches and details to areas too small to be appliquéd.

Using the darning foot and leaving the feed dogs up, slide the quilt "sandwich" under the foot. Set the machine for satin stitch. Start with the satin stitch width set at zero; this will make a straight stitch quilting line. Pull the bobbin thread to the top of the sandwich. (This thread will be clipped off later. It is better to spend a little time now pulling the thread up than a longer time clipping the tangle of thread from the back if this

is not done.) Gently move the sandwich to create the desired line. As you feel the need for a thicker line, slow the movement and slowly increase the width to the desired size. Continue to vary the width, then return to the straight stitch. Quilt each fractured section to the edge. Change the color of the top and bobbin thread often to complement or contrast the fabrics where needed.

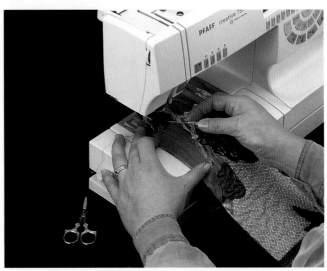

Pull the thread up from the bottom in the beginning to avoid a tangled mess on the back.

SATIN/STRAIGHT QUILTING
ADDS THE DETAIL

Use the same color thread in the bobbin and the top. This eliminates the worry that the bobbin thread is showing on the top, and gives a wonderful pattern and texture to the back of the quilt. The thread should enhance the colors of the quilt.

A long-fiber thread is less likely to cause problems. I like to use Mölnlycke®, Gütermann®, and Mettler. I tend to stay away from the more decorative threads since I have a very low frustration level and I like to sew very fast. These two traits do not work well with the fancy threads.

I store my thread in an old DMC® embroidery thread box. The top drawer has my sky colors, purples and blacks, whites and greys. The second drawer has all the earth and foliage colors, and the bottom drawer has the bobbins and sewing tools. I have over eighty bobbins, with a different color in each.

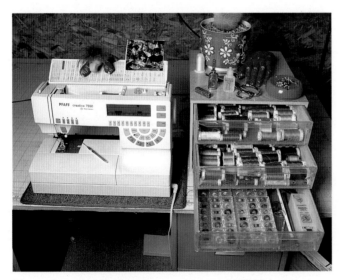

My sewing machine is set up next to an old DMC box that holds my threads and bobbins.

I have noticed it is much easier to get a good flow going with the sewing machine if I sew really fast. You should try it. First take slow, even stitches. Then try to sew faster and go with the rhythm of the machine. I don't believe every stitch needs to be exact. As long as there is not a big difference between the smallest and largest stitch, all the stitches will balance.

Here are some examples of different kinds of Satin/Straight Quilting ideas:

- Edge to edge
- Stipple with zigzag
- Abacus
- Art nouveau
- Undulating
- Snail's trail
- Grass
- Sideways satin stitch for water
- Flowing satin and straight
- Stipple

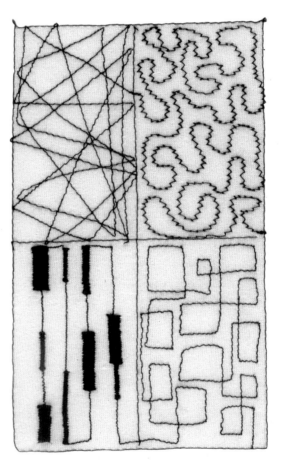

Examples of a few of the fun things you can do with Satin/Straight stitching.

Examples of a few of the fun things you can do with Satin/Straight stitching.

Sometimes I find myself procrastinating before I start to machine quilt. I seem to forget how much fun it is. It is always a long time between quilting one quilt and getting to the quilting stage of the following quilt. But once I sit down at the machine again, in only a minute or two I am tra-la-la-ing along. Don't worry if you don't know what to do. The three of you (you, the machine, and the fabric) will figure out the situation in no time. Remember, "more quilting is better."

It is easy to see each flaw and mistake as you make them. It is as if you are looking through a magnifying glass, seeing in detail the area you are working on. Once the quilt is finished and seen as the "big picture," you won't be able to find the flawed stitches.

Free motion Satin/Straight stitching to create a bed of rocks

A whole cloth sampler of Satin/Straight quilting

TIPS

■ Use a Schmetz Stick Nadel Embroidery needle. Change the needle often. You know the needle is dull when it starts skipping stitches.

■ When threading the sewing machine, make sure the presser lever is in the "up" position. If not, the tension bars are closed and the thread will not be caught in them. This will result in big loops on the bottom.

■ Sewer's Aid® is a silicone product that helps avoid thread breakage. Thread breaks in a machine that has been running for a while and is hot. Run a bead of the silicone along the spool. This will help cool the thread and will also lubricate the inner parts of the machine as the thread moves through.

■ Clean and oil the machine often. Fibers build up in the bottom quickly. A clean machine is a happy machine—which makes for a happy operator.

Canyon, 16" x 16", by Katie. 1994. This is the first piece I did to practice my ten hours of quilting.

■ Ten hours of practice and you will be an expert. Practice. Practice. Use some discarded samples from other projects or an old quilt top you have hidden away to practice on before you create your masterpiece.

A pieced cloth sampler using the print of the fabrics for quilting inspiration

Chapter 13

ASSEMBLING THE QUILT

The sewing line will need to be re-marked on the back of the fractured sections once you have finished quilting; quilting tends to make the section smaller. Trim the excess backing and batting even with the top. Press the quilted piece, starting at the center and working toward the edge.

Return to the foundation copy and discard all the taped-on templates. Cut the foundation copy apart along the fracture lines. Place the foundation copy fracture section on the back of the quilted piece. Mark the sewing line and reference marks. It is possible you will have less than the needed seam allowance. If this happens try pressing the quilted piece again, stretching it to the edge. As long as you have even a wee bit of a seam allowance, it should be OK.

If after pressing and stretching you still have a quilted section that is too small for the paper pattern, mark it as close to the edge as you can. With the wool batting you can still count on steaming and blocking the piece to get it to lie flat. As you work with this method, you will begin to understand all the little things that make the fractured sections smaller and you can improve as you go. The more you do, the better you will get.

Treat the fractured sections as one piece of thick fabric. Pin the sewing lines together every inch or two. Sew right sides together with a smaller than normal stitch. Firmly press the seams open and trim them to an eighth of an inch.

Re-mark the seam and reference marks on the back of the quilted section.

Pin the line and the reference marks with right sides together. Trim seams and press open.

SET-IN CORNERS

Sew one seam to the corner, clip to the seamline, turn the piece, and sew the other seam. Firmly press the seams open and trim them to an eighth of an inch. This helps eliminates bulk.

Turn the edge, make a fold to match the seam to be sewn, pin, and sew.

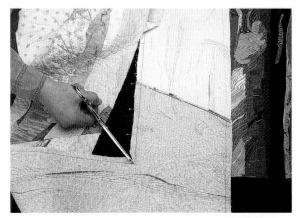

Pin and sew one side of a set-in corner. Clip inside corner to the end of the stitching.

I used set-in corners to finish *Canyon de Chelly* (shown on pages 68–70).

Press the seams open and the corner will be perfect.

FINISHING THE QUILT

The raw seams on the back will be finished with a strip of fabric. Choose a fabric that complements the backing fabrics. Cut it into 1½"-wide bias strips for curved seams and 1½"-wide straight strips for the straight seams. Sew wrong sides together with a ¼" seam. Insert a ½"-wide metal turning bar. (My husband made one for me from an old hacksaw blade he filed down.) Press so the seam is at the back.

Press the seams open.

Lay strips over the seams and baste in place. Hand appliqué on both sides of the strip and be sure none of the stitches show on the front. This is a long and tedious process. The only way I can stand it is to make a nest in my bed with lots of pillows to support my back, rent some videos, and make a day or two of it. I just sew and listen to movies.

Once all the seams are covered, square the outside edge of the quilt. If the quilt doesn't lie flat, steam it first. Lay the quilt flat on the floor. The wool batting will allow you to "block" the piece. You can use a regular steam iron or a professional steamer (the kind that dress shops use to steam their clothes). These can be purchased or rented. Steam the entire surface and leave flat until it is dry. Use a T square to square up all the edges.

I like to have a friend or two, or a husband, around for this part. It can be dreadful when you get all the rulers, T squares, and triangles lined up to prove a square and see you have to cut more than you would like. Actually, cutting off even an inch represents hours of work. But inevitably there will be inches here and there that have to go, and a second opinion is helpful. Prove the square all around the quilt. Slide a rotary mat under the edge of the quilt, have someone else hold the ruler firmly in place, and cut away the excess.

Apply a binding to the edge (1½", folded in half). Machine stitch the binding to the front and hand stitch to the back. Because the finished piece is so heavily quilted, it feels more like canvas than a soft quilt. I like to call them tapestries. They should be rolled to store or transport. If the quilts are creased, they will need to be blocked again.

Strips to cover seams. Press seam to back using a turning bar.

Hand sew strips over seams.

Steam the quilt to make it flat.

The three photos used in *Canyon de Chelly*

Photo of background used
in *Canyon de Chelly*

Drawing of *Canyon de Chelly*

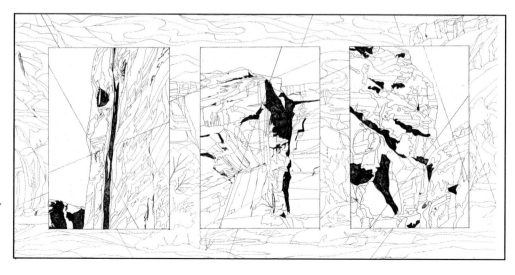

Canyon de Chelly, 96" x 54", by Katie. 1996.

Canyon de Chelly (pronounced *canyon du shay*) is located in
the northeast corner of Arizona on the Navajo Nation. I
photographed it in early November during an excursion
through the canyon. Our Navajo guide told us about the
history, pointed out the petroglyphs, and shared the stories
his grandmother told him about the rock formations.

Back of *Canyon de Chelly*

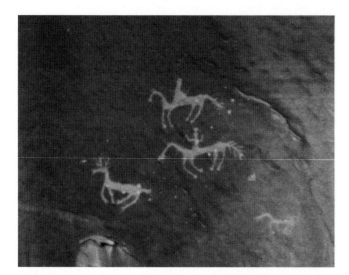

Photo of petroglyph

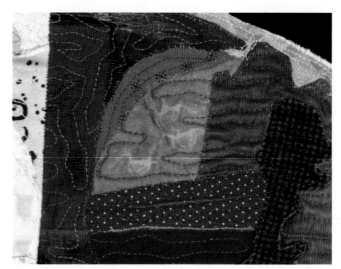

Detail of petroglyph used in quilt

Chapter 14

LABELING THE QUILT

The label on the back of the quilt can tell the story. Tape the original photograph of the landscape onto a piece of paper. Write or type the name of the place, any history or interesting information, your name and address, and the date the quilt was completed. Heat transfer this onto fabric and sew it to the back of the quilt. This makes for an interesting documentation of the journey taken to make the piece.

A PERSONAL REVELATION ON LABELING

I recently lost a quilt in shipping. Eight months later it was found. To make a long, curious story short, I was called one morning by someone from a salvage company. They had bought, sight unseen, the contents of a large salvage truck (salvage from shipping companies, excess inventory, or a number of other possibilities). In the bottom of the truck they found my quilt. The only way they knew to contact me was from the information on the photo transfer label sewn to the back of my quilt. Miracle of miracles—the quilt was returned to its rightful owner.

If you ship your quilts, you are always told to put one label on the outside of the box and one on the inside. How many of us actually put the other label in the box? From now on, I will take this one step further. The label on the box, the label taped to the bag around the quilt, and the label sewn to the quilt will include my name, city, state, and phone number. If the quilt has sold, I will add the phone number of the new owner.

SHIPPING ADVICE

If you ship your quilts UPS, they will insure up to $50,000 if you have an official appraisal. Do not list galleries or quilt show names on the package on the "to" or "from"; only use ordinary names. Send next day delivery, then call the recipient to make sure it arrived.

If you are shipping with Federal Express, take out one-travel-day insurance for that particular package as artwork. Contact Federal Express for the insurance company that handles your area. Send your quilt via overnight delivery and call the recipient to make sure it arrived.

Different labels I have used for the backs of my quilts

STUDENT QUILTS

MCARTHUR-BURNEY FALLS
46" x 57". Linda S. Schmidt, Dublin, California.
Quilt inspired by a photograph taken by Carr Clifton.

"This quilt really is fractured, but you can hardly tell because I kept the fabrics and values consistent between the fractured sections."

WARREN'S DREAM
41" x 60". Nancy Lee Chong, Woodinville, Washington.
Photograph by Mark Frey.

"This fractured riverscape quilt is made entirely by hand appliqué. The design is my interpretation of a poster entitled 'Coming Home-Chinook' by Darrell Davis, a Montana artist. My husband Warren, asked me to make a quilt like the poster, and after the Fractured Landscapes class, I finally had the courage. (I am very proud of this quilt, especially how the larger fish really jump out at the viewer.)"

MENDOCINO ANYTIME
48" x 30". Marge Wood,
Danville, California.

"One of my favorite
views is of the little
village of Mendocino
on the northern coast of
California. Seen from
the bluffs to the south
across the sparkling bay,
perched there above the
cliffs, in sun or fog, or by
starlight, it always makes
me smile."

FRACTURED ROCK
34" x 28". Shirley Connolly,
Atlin, British Columbia.

"The fractured rock on the
beach, with Atlin Lake and
Mountain in the back-
ground, is from a photo
I took near my home in
northern British Columbia.
The fall colors in the willow
leaves frame the right side
of the rock."

THE CHURCH AT TAOS
42" x 40". Narra Gross Tsiagkourts,
Los Alamos, New Mexico.

"This quilt was inspired by a cover of *New Mexico* magazine I had saved for almost 15 years. Finally a use for this inspiration arrived when I took the Fractured Landscape class."

ECLECTIC PUEBLO
46½" x 31". Jacquelyn R. Nouveau,
Chapel Hill, North Carolina.
Quilt inspired by a photograph
taken by Ken Raveill.

"Fracturing with color values and geometric overlays adds a sense of energy to this otherwise placid pueblo scene. For me the pueblo has taken on the vibrancy and dynamics of a Native American powwow."

UNTITLED
"34 x 34". Nicole Dunn,
Los Alamos, New Mexico.

"This quilt was for me
a study in color values.
I tried to create a visually
pleasing and intriguing
3-D image with sand, the
mountains, and light from
the sun."

RIO GRANDE GORGE
40" x 54". Corinne van der Ploeg Nichols,
Santa Fe, New Mexico.

"For years I drove down into the Rio
Grande Gorge, and up again at the other
side of the river to Taos, marveling at the
majestic beauty of the Gorge, and I
wanted to capture this beauty in a quilt."

A GLORIOUS NIGHT
TO REMEMBER
30" x 24½". Maurine Roy,
Edmonds, Washington.
Photograph by Mark Frey.

"*A Glorious Night* . . . is of the
lighthouse at Fort Worden, Point
Townsend, Washington."

UNTITLED
29" x 29". Rhoda Loreergn,
Monroe, Washington.
Photograph by Trygve Hermann.

"I made this as a gift for Shirley
Hermann. This was the most
exciting project I have made.
Thanks, Katie."

LOG CABIN IN THE WOODS
32" x 32". Kathy Smith,
Arlington, Washington.

"This quilt is from a photo
taken of the back view from
my log house. Fracturing
with rectangles in the offset
Log Cabin block simplified
a first project."

VIEW FROM THE TRAIN
37" x 32". Ann Ferkovich,
Santa Fe, New Mexico.

"I took photos on an early
autumn day while riding the
Cumbres Toltec and Scenic
Railroad, a narrow gauge line
between Chama, New Mexico
and Antonito, Colorado. The
grass was already golden; the
firs, perfect pyramids; aspen,
beginning to turn—and it was
all framed by an incredible sky."

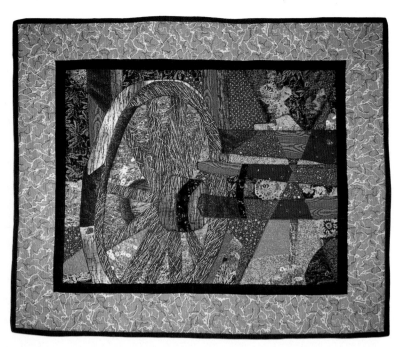

HOPE SPRINGS ETERNAL
36" x 30". Judy Chapen,
Marysville, Washington.

"I took the picture for this quilt
at the Jennings Park Master
Gardener's Garden in Marysville,
Washington. Gardens have always
represented hope to me—and faith
that the cycles of life continue—
that even the man-made structures
left behind (the old wagon) can be
embraced by the natural world
and enhance each other."

NORWEGIAN WATERWHEEL
47" x 47". Ruth West, Pine, Colorado.
Photograph by Ben Blankenburg.

"The photo that was the inspiration for the quilt was taken
by me at the Norwegian Folk Museum in Oslo, Norway.
A picture postcard of an ancient ox cart with wood carvings
was photo transferred to cloth. I used over a dozen different
decorative stitches to appliqué the pieces together."

ARCTIC LIGHT
31" x 39". Becky Sundquist, Pinole, California.
Photograph by Sharon Risedorph.

"This quilt is based on a photograph I took at the Arctic Circle
in Finland. I designed most of the fabric on the computer and
printed directly on silk and cotton. The border was created
from real birch bark by scanning the piece of bark into the
computer and digitally manipulating the image to create a
repeat pattern."

VIEW FROM TALIESIN WEST
46½" x 34". Angie Woolman,
Albany, California.
Photograph by Sharon
Risedorph.

"This is from Frank Lloyd
Wright's Architecture School in
Scottsdale, Arizona. My photo
was taken of the grounds, not
any structures. I think it is
interesting that the fracture
lines I drew resembled some
of the angles which exist in the
actual architecture."

DUSK ON DRIFTWOOD BAY
48½" x 40". Ildiko Francais, Venice, France.

"Katie's workshop has opened whole new horizons for
me. In this wallhanging I tried to convey the serenity and
dramatic beauty of twilight on the Thousand Isles of
Canada. I used my own photos and hand-painted pieces
to achieve transparency. I layered organza in some areas
and used metallic thread as an accent."

PINK FLAMINGOS
21" x 29". Sandi Barrett,
Marlbourough, Massachusetts.

"Lush tropical trees, shallow golden ponds, and
majestic pink flamingos grace St. Thomas, Virgin
Islands, bringing back memories of a Caribbean cruise
I took with my family. It was a bittersweet time in my life
and the fracturing of this picture represents the
different emotions."

VISIONS OF SUNSET
50" x 45". Sue Alfuth-Lamb,
Fond du Lac, Wisconsin.

"*Visions of Sunset* is a view
I have in my head of a place
I can always go to, especially
when I need to get away from
the world. It is made of fabric
dyed especially for this
project by Liz Axford and
Constance Scheele."

END OF THE SHIFT
48" x 32". Kathy Proctor, Snohomish, Washington.

"I enjoyed the class and love this technique."

RAIN FOREST
37" x 44". Laurel Squire,
Mundingburra, Australia.

"My vision of a detail of a rainforest."

LILY
30" x 46". Diana Roberts, Concord, California.

"This wild lily blooms every year in the high
Sierra Mountains on the banks of the
Tuoloumne River. I took the photo looking up
into the flower with the sky behind it. I was
able to create the lily in fabric with Katie's
innovative method."

BRIDAL VEIL MEADOW
39½" x 34½". Norah McMeeking,
Cambridge, England.
Photograph by Gavin McMeeking.

"To fracture this landscape I
pretended I was cropping the
photograph smaller and smaller
until I had just the waterfall in view.
Then I used the cropping lines to
do a value study. I used my son's
photo instead of my own to give
me some emotional distance from
the subject."

TAYLOR PARK RESERVOIR
48½" x 40½". Hope Stauffer,
Steamboat Springs, Colorado.

GRAND CANYON NATIONAL PARK
39½" x 27". Peg Johnson,
Rye, New Hampshire.
Quilt inspired by a photograph
taken by Josiah Davidson.
Photograph by Gary Samson.

"It was so exciting to learn Katie's
Fractured Landscape process! In
making this quilt I used about twenty-
five different colors of thread for the
quilting. As the quilt began to take
shape, I got more and more en-
thused! I thoroughly enjoyed the
whole process."

TARANGIRE BAOBAB
44" x 31½". Joyce Trompa, Dar Salaam, Tanzania.

"I live in Tanzania, a beautiful country in East Africa, where the
magical Baobab tree is found abundantly, especially in the
northern parts such as Tarangire. In many African traditions it
is a sacred tree where people come to worship. There is a
Kiswahili saying: Kila shetani na myuya wake, 'Every spirit has
its Baobab.' There is also a custom to tie a scrap of fabric or
thread to the tree and make a wish. I also felt a special energy
from these trees which I tried to convey in my quilt. It has
mostly hand-dyed and local African fabrics."

HOLLAND QUILT
25½" x 31¼". Kathy DesRoches, Rochester, New Hampshire.
Photograph by Lisa A. Nugent

"I've always had a fascination with landscape quilts, but the
method of making landscape quilts fought my natural
tendency to work improvisationally. I became very excited
as I pieced the first section of this quilt, and my excitement
grew from quilting it and eventually putting the fractured
sections together."

BALI LEAVES
40" x 29". Shirley Connolly,
Atlin, British Columbia.

"While in Bali, I sketched these tropical leaves. The quilt is completely made from Balinese fabrics. The black and white binding represents the traditional Bali belief of good and evil."

WAPITI IN THE HIGH COUNTRY
55½" x 44". Cathy Anderson, Los Alamos, New Mexico.

"This quilt depicts the beauty of New Mexico's majestic mountains and wildlife, and the diverse culture—represented by the fracturing of the Native American pottery."

THE SOURCE
80" x 94". Susan Lea Hackett, Alameda, California.

"I covered my design wall with vellum, drew in the fracture lines, and then sketched in the major shapes vaguely. I cut on the fracture lines to make large templates, "free-hand" crazy piecing each area and replacing it on the wall before moving on. No smaller templates were used, and all shapes were pieced—no appliqué."

WINTER ON LONG ISLAND
36" x 32". Lynne Douglas, Sonoma, California.

"The barn reminds me of the wonderful, snowy winters I spent with my family on the east end of Long Island."

PAYETTE RIVER LANDSCAPE
31" x 38". Linda Roby, Boise, Idaho.
Photograph by Neal E. Collett.

"Creating landscape quilts lets me combine my interests in photography and quilting with my appreciation of nature. I enjoy the process of starting with a large scale composition and ending with the detailed texture of elements such as rocks and plants."

ARCHED BRIDGE
38" x 31". Susanne Gregg, Glencoe, Illinois.

"In Japan, the arched bridge symbolizes the difficult path from this world to paradise, while the pine tree represents longevity. This bridge leads to the Japanese garden at the Chicago Botanic Garden in Glencoe, Illinois. I photographed the scene immediately following the last snowfall of the '95 winter season."

GHOST RANCH REVISITED
44" x 23". Judi Wagner, Fernandino Beach, Florida.

"I come to quilting as a professional painter. Putting my photos of clouds, earth, and trees on fabric, and inserting them in the composition, the landscape becomes more abstract in nature."

FAIRFIELD COUNTY FAIRGROUNDS
38" x 30". Karen Davis, Lancaster, Ohio.

"These fairgrounds are the oldest working grounds, with original buildings, in Ohio."

BADLANDS, SOUTH DAKOTA
45" x 36". Janet Sorell, Oakland, California.

"Taste the burning Badlands Wind,
Feel it swirl inside.
Swallow up a soaring wing
And hang on for the ride.
Katie helped me shape this feeling,
Fracturing fabric, laying the land.
Bringing back the warm sensation
With her kind and helping hand."

PFEIFFER BEACH
36" x 35". Donalene Rasmussen,
San Diego, California.

"I was taken by the extreme beauty
of this beach at sunset. The rock
formations silhouetted against the
yellows of the sky and water
provided an inspiring composition.
I love portraying my native state
of California."

DESERT SEASONS
39" x 31". Betty Johnson, Dayton, Ohio.
Photograph by G. Frank Johnson.

"I was awed by the beauty and colors of Coral Pink Sand
Dunes State Park, Utah, even on a winter visit. I decided to
use photographs my husband took as a basis for the
landscape, fracturing the areas to show how the desert
comes alive with bloom in another season."

BLUE MOUNTAIN QUILT
39" x 39". Phyllis B. Holland, Los Alamos, New Mexico.

"After years of quiltmaking, I enjoyed the challenges of
Katie's technique. It opens up a new universe of ideas for
future quilts."

DATIL MOUNTAINS,
WOODCUTTERS' PARADISE
57" x 37". Patricia Heydt,
Albuquerque, New Mexico.
Photograph by Raymond C. Nelson.

"The actual mountain skyline was
traced from a projected slide. Using
the freezer paper method, I worked in
a rather free-form way by changing
many elements as the piece evolved,
and experimenting with a variety of
machine stitching and dimensional
techniques."

MOUNT DIABLO FOOTHILLS
44" x 32". Dena Canty, Piedmont, California.

"This is a view of the Mount Diablo foothills near my home.
I used Katie's appliqué techniques, but did not choose the
"quilt-as-you-go" method, since the piece only measured
44" x 32"."

LAKE POWELL MEMORIES II; RAINBOW BRIDGE
31" x 42". Fran Wilson, Savannah, Georgia.

"I had no idea I was capable of doing a landscape like this,
since I can't draw. But with this technique, you don't need to
be able to draw, you just need to be able to see."

MOTHER HUMMINGBIRD
39½" x 23½". Ginny Eckley, Kingwood, Texas.

"This female of the Calypte Anna species stays busy feeding her two young fledglings. Her own needs call for a daily food allowance greater than her body weight. She is surrounded by blooming Trumpet Vine, which provides the nectar needed to feed her young."

ALPINE GLOW
33" x 27". Jo Morrison, Steamboat Springs, Colorado.

"We enjoy watching the evening alpine glow on Mount Werener from our living room, so it seemed really fitting that I try to capture the wonderful colors as my first fractured landscape."

CHANCE ENCOUNTER
22½" x 34". Lynn Lichtenstern, San Diego, California.

Finding this photo was a chance encounter for me, as was wildlife photographer Tom Leeson's chance encounter with the red fox.

THE PROJECT

This pattern is called Seasons. It can be adapted to any season you choose. The following instructions will be a review of "The Process" at the front of the book and of the previous chapters. We will skip steps 1 through 3 and go directly to step 4.

4. **Enlarging the Drawing:** Take this pattern to a print shop and have them enlarge it to any size you desire. The examples shown were enlarged to approximately 13" x 17", but any size will work. Make three copies of the enlarged pattern. Also make three or four copies of the fracture map on page 92 for shading.

    Spray mount one copy to a piece of railroad board. Staple another copy to a pin-up surface. Put the last copy aside to use later with the stabilizer. Cut apart the cardboard copy into fracture sections and staple the sections to the pin-up surface.

5. **Shading the Fractures:** Decide on the values of the fractures by shading the fracture maps. Leave the light section blank; shade the medium sections with pencil and the dark sections with black pen. Try three or four variations and choose the one that pleases you most.

6. **Sorting the Fabrics:** Sort your fabrics into 7 steps, starting with white and lights in step 1 and continuing through black and dark fabrics in step 7. Steps 2 through 6 will be values from light to dark. Use the charts on the sides of the color pages as aids.

SPRING
17" x 13".
Hazel Brooks,
Paso Robles, California.

7. **Marking the Templates:** Choose a fracture section. Outline the edge with a colored pencil. Indicate color and value on each template.

8. **Cutting It Out:** Check the shading map to determine the value of the section. Indicate those steps needed from your seven steps. Cut a shape from the section, choose the fabric, and mark the template shape on the back of the fabric. Cut out the fabric. Staple the template behind the fabric in position on the pin-up wall. Do this for each fractured section.

SUMMER
17" x 13".
Lois K. Regan,
Bakersfield, California.

9. **Turning the Edges:** Use the foundation copy to trace the fractured section of the pattern onto the Sulky stabilizer. Be sure to have the smooth side up. Remove a piece of fabric and the template from the wall. Spray the back of the fabric with starch and lay the template in place. Use a stiletto and iron to fold the fabric over the template. Remove the template and heat set the fabric onto the stabilizer. Continue in this manner until all the pieces are in place on the stabilizer. Turn the whole thing over and heat set everything in place. Continue with the other fractured sections

Take this pattern to a printer to have enlarged to your desired size. (See photocopy permission on page 2.)

AUTUMN
17" x 13".
Sevill Preddy,
San Luis Obispo, California.

WINTER
17" x 13".
Lorna Morck,
Solvang, California.

10. **Machine Appliqué:** Set your machine to blind hem. Using transparent thread in the top and a neutral colored thread in the bobbin, stitch all the pieces in place. Remove the stabilizer.

11. **Basting and Backing:** Cut batting and backing for each section. Spray baste the batting and smooth the top and bottom in place.

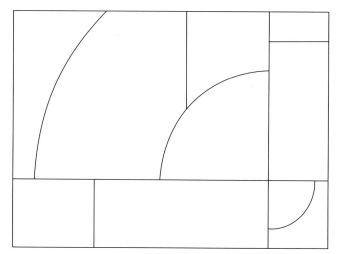

Make several copies of this fracture map to shade. (See photocopy permission on page 2.)

12. **Machine Quilting:** Set your machine to zigzag, use the darning foot, and leave the feed dogs up. Vary the stitch width from single stitch to satin stitch to add texture and design to your quilt.

13. **Assembling the Quilt:** Trim the excess backing and batting from each fractured section. Return to the foundation copy and cut the sections apart. Re-mark the sewing line on the back of each section, pin the sewing line to match both sides, and sew the sections, right sides together. Press seams open firmly. Apply bias or straight grain tape over the raw seams after they have been trimmed to 1/8". Hand appliqué in place. Press the complete piece flat, square the edges, and apply a binding.

14. **Labeling the Quilt:** Make a label and apply it to the back.

Congratulations! You are now ready to try one on your own. Grab your camera, go find a beautiful place, and start planning your next quilt. Have fun.

APPENDIX

The following credits are for the student quilts shown at the bottom of pages 14–15 and 94–95 (reading from left to right):

NAVY LAKE
11" x 8½"
Lynne Lichtenstern
San Diego, California

YOSEMITE MEMORIES
7" x 8½"
Carla R. Martinez
Ramona, California

OREGON COAST
10" x 8"
Doris E. Williams
Arnold, California

VALLEY TULIPS
11½" x 9½"
Susan Wells Hall
Mount Vernon, Washington

BEACH HOUSE
8" x 10"
Gail Bartlett
Corvallis, Oregon

HAPPY TRAILS
8½" x 8"
Susan Estabrook
Bolton, CANADA

UNTITLED
12" x 8½"
Jan P. Krentz
Lemoore, California

MOJAVE
12" x 14"
Sandy Bosley
Ridgecrest, California

MEADOWS AND MOUN-
TAINS
9" x 9"
Mariane Jolly
Castro Valley, California

MINI GRAND CANYON
8" x 8"
Leigh Martin
Jerome, Arizona

UNTITLED
13" x 12"
Andree Gnudde
BELGIUM

FLAMINGOS OF LAKE
BOGORIA
13" x 10½"
Renee M. Solomon
Arnold, California

LESSON #1
10" x 8"
Grace M. Crocker
Glenn, California

COLORADO PINE
9" x 11"
Paula K. Miller
Parker, Colorado

MY GUY
10" x 11"
Ellen Aase
NORWAY

GUM TREES
12" x 10"
Philena L. Richards
Newcastle, Maine

The following credits are for the student quilts shown at the beginning of each chapter in the upper left corners:

Chapter 1
HOWE SOUND
8½" x 11". Deborah Hollister,
Lake Oswego, Oregon.

Chapter 2
UNTITLED
8" x 8". Mary K. Hitchner
Haverford, Pennsylvania.

Chapter 3
OLD DEAD TREE
17" x 13". Linda S. Schmidt,
Dublin, California.

Chapter 4
EARLY LIGHT
16½" x 14½". Mary S. Moore,
Crawfordsville, Indiana.

Chapter 5
SUNRISE ON THE SHORE
12½" x 8½".
Judy A. Gorrindo,
Santa Barbara, California.

Chapter 6
A VIEW OF THE PEAK
13" x 11". Cheryl Porter,
Wheaton, Illinois.

Chapter 7
STOW LAKE, GOLDEN
GATE PARK
11" x 15". Donna Butts,
Oakhurst, California.

Chapter 8
SUNRISE
11" x 13½". Kelly Simbirdi,
San Carlos, California.

Chapter 9
FRACTURED 'SCAPE
A LA KATIE
12" x 15". Christy White,
Los Altos, California.

Chapter 10
BOTH SIDES NOW
14" x 11". Rita Kilstrom,
Arnold, California.

Chapter 11
FRACTURED LANDSCAPE
11½" x 14½". Lois Worell,
Falcon, Missouri.

Chapter 12
ALI'S CANYON
9" x 11". Mandy Munroe,
Randolf, New Jersey.
Photograph by Vicki Clauss.

Chapter 13
RED ROCKS REVISITED
8" x 8". Judy Smith-Kressley,
Strafford, Pennsylvania.

Chapter 14
RED ROCK CANYON,
SIMPLIFIED
10" x 11". Karen Michaels,
Hayward, California.

Student Quilts
UNTITLED
34" x 17".
Julie Klaes Bradley,
Walpole, Massachusetts.

The Project
WINTER
25" x 18".
By Katie,
Santa Fe, New Mexico.

BIBLIOGRAPHY

Adams, Ansel. *Examples: The Making of 40 Photographs*. Boston: Little, Brown & Co., 1983.

Adams, Ansel. *The New Ansel Adams Photography Series: Book 1: The Camera; Book 2: The Negative; Book 3: The Print*. Boston: Little, Brown & Co., 1983.

Heinemann, Bruce W. *A Guide to Photographing the Art of Nature*. Seattle: Prior Publishing, 1994.

Sussman, Aaron. *The Amateur Photographer's Handbook*. New York: Thomas Y. Crowell Company, 1973.

Thornton, Gene. Introductory essay in *Landscape Photography: The Art and Techniques of Eight Modern Masters*. New York: Amphoto, an imprint of Watson-Guptill Publications, 1984.

Wagner, Judi, and Tony Van Hasselt. *Painting with the White of Your Paper*. Cincinnati: North Light Books, 1994.

OTHER BOOKS BY C&T

Art & Inspiration: Ruth B. McDowell, Ruth B. McDowell
The Art of Silk Ribbon Embroidery, Judith Baker Montano
Beyond the Horizon, Small Landscape Appliqué, Valerie Hearder
Buttonhole Stitch Appliqué, Jean Wells
Colors Changing Hue, Yvonne Porcella
Crazy with Cotton, Diana Leone
Elegant Stitches: An Illustrated Stitch Guide & Source Book of Inspiration, Judith Baker Montano
Everything Flowers, Quilts from the Garden, Jean and Valori Wells
The Fabric Makes the Quilt, Roberta Horton
Faces & Places, Images in Appliqué, Charlotte Warr Andersen
Heirloom Machine Quilting, Harriet Hargrave
Kaleidoscopes & Quilts, Paula Nadelstern
Impressionist Quilts, Gai Perry
Landscapes & Illusions, Joen Wolfrom
The Magical Effects of Color, Joen Wolfrom
Mariner's Compass Quilts, New Directions, Judy Mathieson
Mastering Machine Appliqué, Harriet Hargrave
Nancy Crow: Improvisational Quilts, Nancy Crow
Patchwork Quilts Made Easy, Jean Wells (co-published with Rodale Press, Inc.)
Quilts, Quilts, and More Quilts! Diana McClun and Laura Nownes
Schoolhouse Appliqué: Reverse Techniques and More, Charlotte Patera
Simply Stars, Alex Anderson
Small Scale Quiltmaking: Precision, Proportion, and Detail, Sally Collins
Soft-Edge Piecing, Jinny Beyer
Stripes in Quilts, Mary Mashuta
Symmetry: A Design System for Quiltmakers, Ruth B. McDowell
3 Dimensional Design, Katie Pasquini
Tradition with a Twist: Variations on Your Favorite Quilts, Blanche Young and Dalene Young Stone
Trapunto by Machine, Hari Walner
Visions: QuiltArt, Quilt San Diego
The Visual Dance: Creating Spectacular Quilts, Joen Wolfrom

For more information write for a free catalog from:

C&T Publishing
P.O. Box 1456
Lafayette, CA 94549
(1-800-284-1114)

INDEX

Contributing Quiltmakers

ABOUT THE AUTHOR

Katie Pasquini Masopust began her art career at a very young age. From her early interest in painting, she quickly developed a talent for quiltmaking. Beginning with traditional quilts, her techniques evolved into mandala-style, three-dimensional, and isometric perspective quilts. Her latest work, fractured landscapes, combines the organic quality of the landscape with the structure and geometry of her earlier works. Her creativity and willingness to try new things have been the hallmarks of her success.

A teacher since 1981, Katie has now taught her innovative techniques to thousands of students around the world. Her energy and enthusiasm make her classes both fun and educational.

Katie has won many awards throughout her career but considers Best of Show at the Houston Quilt Festival in 1982 and 1986 and at the Pacific International Quilt Show in 1994, and First and Second Place at the American Quilters Society show in 1995 her best achievements.

Her work has also appeared in *Quilter's® Newsletter Magazine*, *American Quilter*, *Fiber Arts*, and other publications. In addition to *Fractured Landscape Quilts*, Katie is the author of *Mandala*, *The Contemporary Sampler*, *3 Dimensional Design*, and *Isometric Perspective*.

Katie lives with her family in Santa Fe, New Mexico.